Alesia family

Santa's Christmas Journey

Roger Brooke

Illustrated by Elizabeth J. Miles

Rand McNally & Company
Chicago • New York • San Francisco

This is the story of how once a year
I fly round the world with eight trusty reindeer.
And bring to each child in each house in each land
A wrapped Christmas present, delivered by hand.

Of course there are secrets that I cannot tell—
Like the specially marvelous magical spell
That I cast when I order my reindeer to fly
Several hundreds of miles in the blink of an eye . . .
Or the trick that I use when I make myself thin
If a chimney's so small it's too tight to get in,
And another if there is no chimney at all,
When I squeeze through a keyhole and into a hall.

And I can't tell you how I get zillions of toys
   For millions and millions of good girls and boys
On just one little sleigh. But I'll tell you this much,
As I load on each present I squeeze it a touch,
And—presto!—it shrinks to the size of a pea,
So small that it's not always easy to see.
And, of course, as I pull each one out of the sack,
With my next bit of magic the right size comes back!

By the way, I expect you have probably guessed
That of all of my magic the trick that's the best
Is the way that I know just where all of you live
And exactly what each of you wants me to give.
My magic address book knows just where you are,
And it knows if you wished for a doll or a car.
It remembers your brothers and sisters as well,
Though just how it works I'm afraid I won't tell.

Well, last year there were so many presents to bring—
And one of the bells on our sleigh wouldn't ring—
That we left the North Pole rather flustered and late,
And were still over Finland at quarter past eight.

Then Sweden and Norway and Denmark were slow,
As we searched for small villages hidden by snow.
The Netherlands greeted our coming with rain.
It was pouring in France. There were hailstorms in Spain.
And although I had hoped to leave Europe by seven,
We didn't reach England till nearly eleven.

We flew up the Thames coming in from the west—
Checked the time by **Big Ben** (that's the clock
  I like best)—
Then right to my work. Into each London house
I crept with my presents, as still as a mouse.
I stopped at each hospital, inn, and hotel,
And filled everyone's stocking swiftly and well,
Then out of the city, to Cornwall to Wales,
To each waiting cottage, through snowstorms and gales.
Northward to Scotland we flew like a feather
And found every farmhouse—in spite of the weather.

After Ireland we swooped to the Rock of Gibraltar,
Then sailed on a wind to the island of Malta.
Over African jungles the stars, softly gleaming,
Showed us animal families peacefully dreaming.
By the time we hit Cape Town the night air was hot.
Did I need my fur coat? Why, most certainly not!

Then across the Atlantic to raging Cape Horn,
And on up to Rio at two in the morn.
I know that the children asleep in Brazil
Would have left me hot coffee to keep out the chill.
As we passed Puerto Rico I reached in my sack
To give my good reindeer their half-way-round snack.
"We must build up our strength for our journey," I said,
"North America's next, and there's hard work ahead!"

Canada was first—and from Montreal west
We stopped at each housetop with never a rest,
Till at last in Vancouver we hurtled around
And raced back to Toronto in one mighty bound.
"Now on to the States!" There were ice storms and frost,
And a sackful of toys very nearly was lost
When it fell off the sleigh as we hit bumpy ground
Coming in through a blizzard on Long Island Sound.
Skyscrapers, houses, big families and small—
We whirled round New York with surprises for all.
Upstairs and downstairs I raced with my pack,
While my good reindeer rested until I came back.

634

T hen southward we dashed, making many a call
(Though just north of Pittsburgh I took quite a fall).
At three the moon rose in the east, which was lucky,
For it lit our way over the hills of Kentucky.
We whisked through Chicago, and on to the West,
Crossed Nebraska and Utah with never a rest—
Up and down California, then onward we flew,
With the ocean beneath us and much still to do.

All America's children were given their toys—
All those millions of girls and those millions of boys.
When at last we had finished I waved them good-bye
Including one smart little girl in Hawaii
Who had been rather naughty and not gone to sleep
But had opened one eye as I started to creep
To her stocking. Now, peeping's forbidden, you see,
So with one magic word—it's known only to me—
I sent her to sleep, making sure it would seem
That her seeing me there had just been a nice dream.

On, onward we raced, now our speed was terrific.
In twenty-five seconds we crossed the Pacific
To New Guinea, New Zealand, and westward once more,
To arrive in Australia at four thirty-four.
Out there Christmas comes in the summer, so we
Parked our sleigh on the beach and cooled off in the sea.
Next off to the north through Hong Kong and Japan,
Then back across India and Afghanistan.
Now at last my brave reindeer were tired and worn
As we flew up Arabia into the dawn.